BEASTLY!

There are plenty of cute and cuddly animals in the world. But there are just as many killer critters that would rather eat you than snuggle.

I'M NOT CUTE! I AM A BEAST!

CONTENTS

Beastly! 4

Awful African Wild Dogs. 6

Horrible Hippopotamuses 8

Scary Saltwater Crocodiles 10

Sinister Saw-Scaled Vipers 12

Monstrous Mantises 14

Killer Geography Cone Snails 16

Beastly Blue-Ringed Octopuses. . . 18

Ghastly Great White Sharks 20

Curious Killer Critters 22

Glossary. 24

Index 24

Credits

Images are courtesy of Shutterstock.com. With thanks to GettyImages, ThinkstockPhoto, and iStockphoto.

Cover Vector_Up, irin-k, Eric Isslee. Recurring images gravity_point, 8–9 Francisco Blanco, Svetlana Foote. 10–11, aaltair, Ekaterina Chudakova, frank60, photowind. 12–13 Emőke Dénes (Wikimedia Commons), Jose Barquero. J. 14–15 Jesus Cobaleda, Nick Pecker. 16–17 Agnieszka Bacal, Debbie Steinhausser, Anna Violet. 18–19 Agami Photo Agency, John Navajo, Vishnevskiy Vasily. 20–21 Chanasid kaewpirun, Novim images. 22–23 Keri Delaney, Rob Hainer.

Library of Congress Cataloging-in-Publication Data

Names: Mather, Charis, 1999- author.
Title: Killer critters / by Charis Mather.
Description: Minneapolis, Minnesota : Bearport Publishing Company, [2024] |
    Series: Beastly wildlife | Includes index.
Identifiers: LCCN 2023031003 (print) | LCCN 2023031004 (ebook) | ISBN
    9798889163404 (hardcover) | ISBN 9798889163459 (paperback) | ISBN
    9798889163497 (ebook)
Subjects: LCSH: Dangerous animals--Juvenile literature. | Dangerous aquatic
    animals--Juvenile literature. | Poisonous animals--Juvenile literature.
Classification: LCC QL100 .M375 2024 (print) | LCC QL100 (ebook) | DDC
    591.6/5--dc23/eng/20230712
LC record available at https://lccn.loc.gov/2023031003
LC ebook record available at https://lccn.loc.gov/2023031004

For more information, write to Bearport Publishing, 5357 Penn Avenue South, Minneapolis, MN 55419.

KILLER CRITTERS

by
Charis Mather

BEARPORT
PUBLISHING

Minneapolis, Minnesota

You don't want to get too close to some of the world's most powerful **predators**. It's best to just stick to reading about these brutal beasts!

AWFUL AFRICAN WILD DOGS

I LOVE A PACK LUNCH!

African wild dogs live in groups called packs. Together, they are some of the deadliest hunters in the animal world. Very few creatures can escape a pack of hungry African wild dogs.

African wild dogs work together to take down **prey** much larger than themselves. Watch out, wildebeests and antelopes! The dogs are also known to catch smaller creatures, such as birds and rats.

A wildebeest

African wild dogs

HORRIBLE
HIPPOPOTAMUSES

KEEP OFF THE GRASS. . . . OR ELSE!

Hippopotamuses are some of the deadliest animals on land. They can weigh more than 7,000 pounds (3,200 kg) and are surprisingly fast for their size. Hippos attack hundreds of people every year while protecting their homes.

Hippos spend most of the day in water where they are just as dangerous. They can hold their breath underwater for five minutes. Sometimes, hippos make deadly surprise attacks on boats and other animals in the water.

Hippos can open their mouths more than 4 feet (1 m) wide.

SCARY SALTWATER
CROCODILES

Saltwater crocodiles might be some of the scariest creatures around. They can grow to be about 23 ft (7 m) long. These large animals are able to eat their prey whole. . . . even human-sized prey!

Saltwater crocodiles have one of the strongest bites in the world.

Sometimes, crocs use a move called the death roll. They grab hold of their prey and drag it under the water. Then, the crocs spin quickly to tear the prey apart. *Ouch!*

SINISTER SAW-SCALED

VIPERS

Saw-scaled vipers aren't the biggest or the most **venomous** snakes. However, they may be the deadliest! These snakes often attack humans for almost no reason.

If you live somewhere with lots of saw-scaled vipers, be sure to listen carefully in the evening when these snakes are active. They rub their scales together as a warning to anything that gets too close. *Buzzz!* Beware of strange sounds in the dark!

SSSTAY AWAY!

13

MONSTROUS MANTISES

Praying mantises look ready to fight just about anyone. Their quick **reflexes** and spiked legs make them great predators. Thankfully, they aren't dangerous to humans.

FIGHT ME! I DARE YOU.

14

Bugs, however, *are* on the menu. But the killing doesn't stop there. Praying mantises will also take on larger creatures, such as snakes and birds. Sometimes, **female** mantises even eat their own **mates**.

HONEY, WHAT DID I EVER DO TO YOU?

KILLER GEOGRAPHY CONE
SNAILS

There are few sea critters as slow and as deadly as geography cone snails. Look out! Their stings are venomous enough to kill humans.

When a cone snail attacks, it shoots a spike out of its body that hooks into prey. Dangerous venom **paralyzes** the prey. Then, the snail pulls the spike back toward itself with the meal attached. It's the snail's snack time

The deadly spike comes out of the cone snail's mouth.

BEASTLY BLUE-RINGED
OCTOPUSES

Don't be fooled by how cute blue-ringed octopuses look. These golf ball-sized animals are some of the deadliest ocean creatures. Each one has enough venom to kill a human 26 times. Wow!

Most of the time, it's hard to spot these tiny octopuses. They only show their bright blue rings when they sense danger.

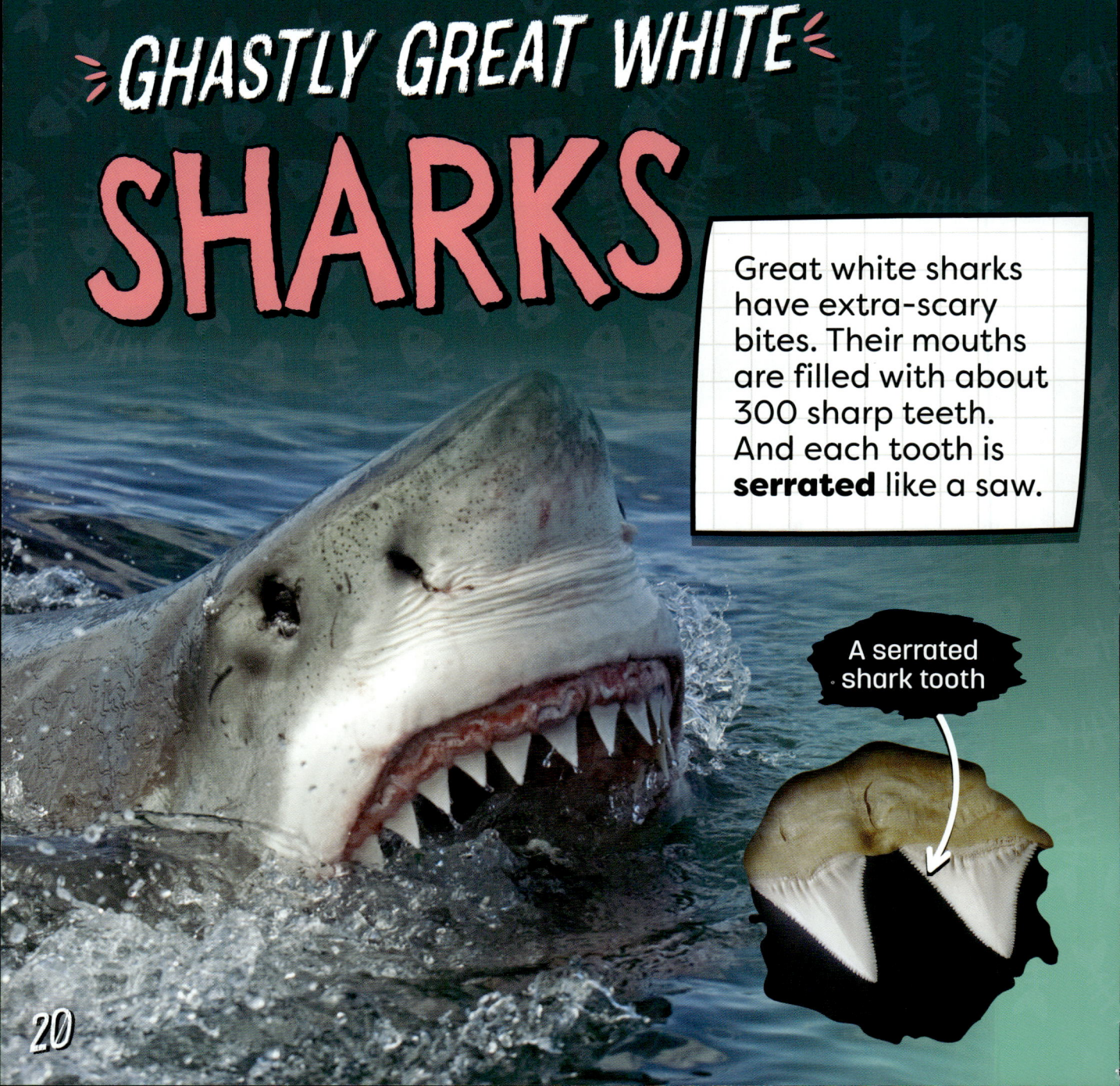

GHASTLY GREAT WHITE
SHARKS

Great white sharks have extra-scary bites. Their mouths are filled with about 300 sharp teeth. And each tooth is **serrated** like a saw.

A serrated shark tooth

20

COME ON, JUST LET ME HAVE A TASTE!

These deadly sharks are picky and sometimes take a test bite. *Crunch!* If their food doesn't taste like a healthy meal, the sharks may let the animal go. Thankfully, these beasts don't usually find humans to be a good snack.

CURIOUS KILLER
CRITTERS

Whether on land or under the sea, there are some mean critters in the world. It can be easy to forget just how beastly some animals are. Sometimes, those teeth are not just for show!

MY TEETH ARE DEFINITELY FOR SHOW.

As scary as these killer critters might be, they are only doing what they need to do to survive. After all, everyone has to eat! Just be glad they are not eating you. . . .

MY BITE ISN'T THAT BEASTLY!

GLOSSARY

female an animal that can have young

mates partners that come together to have babies

paralyzes causes something to be unable to move

predators animals that hunt and eat other animals

prey animals that are eaten by other animals

reflexes actions that happen very quickly without thinking

serrated having sharp, jagged edges

venomous able to poison another creature with a bite, scratch, or stinger

INDEX

bite 10, 20-21, 23
legs 14
packs 6
predators 5, 14
prey 7, 10-11, 17

scales 12-13
spikes 14, 17
teeth 20, 22
venom 12, 16-18
water 9, 11